SOIL

A Follett Beginning SCIENCE Book

SCIENCE EDUCATION CONSULTANTS

EDWARD VICTOR, Ed.D.
PROFESSOR OF SCIENCE EDUCATION
NORTHWESTERN UNIVERSITY

CURTIS MELNICK, Ed.D.
DISTRICT SUPERINTENDENT OF SCHOOLS
CHICAGO PUBLIC SCHOOLS

READING CONSULTANT

JEANNE S. BROUILLETTE
CURRICULUM COORDINATOR
EVANSTON ELEMENTARY SCHOOLS

TECHNICAL CONSULTANT

ROBERT E. TAYLOR
PROFESSOR OF AGRICULTURAL EDUCATION
OHIO STATE UNIVERSITY

TESTED IN THE PUBLIC SCHOOLS

SOIL

RICHARD CROMER

Illustrated by Robert J. Lee

Follett Publishing Company   *Chicago · New York*

Library of Congress Catalog Card Number: AC66-10623

FIRST PRINTING   TLA 8175

WATER
makes soil moist. Plants
cannot grow in soil
without water.

AIR
is found between the
bits of soil. Dry, hard
soil without much air
is not good for plants.

Soil is made up of many different things.
Part of it is rock and rock dust.   This is called
inorganic matter, meaning matter that was never
alive.   Air and water are also inorganic matter.
They, too, are part of the soil.

4

DEAD ORGANIC MATTER slowly turns into a dark material called humus, an important part of the soil.

LIVING ORGANIC MATTER such as roots, small underground plants, and small underground animals are part of the soil.

ROCK MATTER in the soil can be as fine as dust or in the form of large chunks.

U. S. 1697264

Soil also has organic matter in it. The organic matter is either alive now, or else it was once alive. Many tiny living plants and animals are part of the soil. The roots of larger plants are part of the soil. Bits of dead plants and dead animals are also organic matter, and an important part of the soil.

A soil that is a mixture of sand, silt, and clay is called loam. Loam with organic matter in it is soft and easy to work with. It is called mellow loam.

Soils are formed mostly from rocks that have broken up into smaller and smaller pieces. The largest pieces are called gravel. Pieces somewhat smaller are called sand. The next smallest pieces are called silt. The smallest pieces of all are called clay.

Most soils are a mixture of gravel, sand, silt, and clay.

Soil is deep in some places and thin in other places. Often the soil has layers. The picture shows soil layers that can sometimes be seen as one digs into the earth.

The layers are topsoil, subsoil, soil parent material, and bedrock.

TOPSOIL
- darkest in color
- has many living things
- has much organic matter
- has much plant food

SUBSOIL
- lighter in color
- has fewer living things
- has less organic matter
- has little plant food

SOIL PARENT MATERIAL
- made of rock dust, gravel
- has no living things
- has no organic matter
- is formed as bedrock breaks

BEDROCK
- a hard layer of rock
- has many cracks
- breaks up slowly
- changes to soil parent material

HEATING AND COOLING BREAKS ROCK

Rocks are warmed by the sun and get bigger, or expand.

At night, they cool and get smaller, or contract.

The rock cracks and slowly breaks up.

FREEZING AND THAWING BREAKS ROCK

Water fills cracks in the rock.

When water freezes, it expands.

Expanding water can crack rock.

WETTING AND DRYING BREAKS ROCK

Bits of rock swell when they get wet.

When they dry, they get smaller again.

After awhile, the rock crumbles.

Many forces act on solid rock to break it up and form soil. Sunshine, rain, wind, and frost all can break rock. The action of breaking up rock is called weathering. It may take a hundred or a thousand years for weathering to make one inch of soil.

8

MOVING WATER BREAKS ROCK

Streams tumble rocks underwater.

Seas and lakes wear away rock with waves.

Raindrops can break some rocks after a long time.

WIND AND ICE BREAK ROCK

Wind dashes bits of rock against one another.

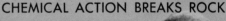

Glaciers are rivers of ice. They move pieces of rock along the land like giant sandpaper and wear away the bedrock.

CHEMICAL ACTION BREAKS ROCK

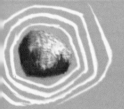

Water dissolves some rock.

Oxygen in the air makes some rock change and crumble.

Ground water has chemicals in it that help dissolve some kinds of rocks.

The longer the weathering goes on, the smaller the pieces of soil will be.

Not all kinds of rock will wear down in the same way. Some kinds are much softer than others and break up much more quickly. In some climates, weathering is very fast.

9

Soil is moved from place to place by water and by winds. Gravity pulls bits of soil downhill and fills in valleys. Slowly the land grows flatter and flatter.

Many kinds of soil in North America were not formed from the rocks just beneath them. Some soils and soil parent materials have been moved to their present place by the same forces that helped make them. Soils are sometimes moved by water, wind, glaciers, and the pull of the earth's gravity.

As soils are moved, they are mixed. And so a cupful of soil from almost anywhere is likely to be made up of many different soils from far-away places.

Glaciers drag along soil and rock as they move. These ice rivers covered about half of North America long, long ago and helped to mix soil.

Tree roots can crack large rocks.

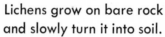

Lichens grow on bare rock
and slowly turn it into soil.

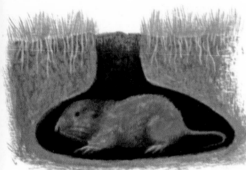

Animals make holes in the ground
and let air in. The air changes the soil.

Living things also help to make soil.
Plant roots are very strong.   As they grow,
they are able to break up rocks.

Tiny plants, called lichens, make a
chemical that helps to break up rock.

Insects, worms, snakes, ground squirrels,
and many other animals help change the soil.

12

Some organic matter in the soil comes from dead plants and animals. When a plant or an animal dies, it begins to decay. Decay bacteria are very tiny living things that change dead things into chemicals that plants can use to make food. Partly decayed plant and animal material is called humus. It gives a dark color to the soil. Humus is a storehouse of chemicals for growing plants. It also helps keep the soil from getting too hard and saves moisture.

1 When plants and animals die, their bodies return to the soil.

2 Decay bacteria, fungi, and other plants act on the dead bodies.

4 After a while, nothing is left but humus, which is slowly changed to chemicals.

3 Insects, worms, and other small animals help take apart bodies.

Where do plants get the elements they need?

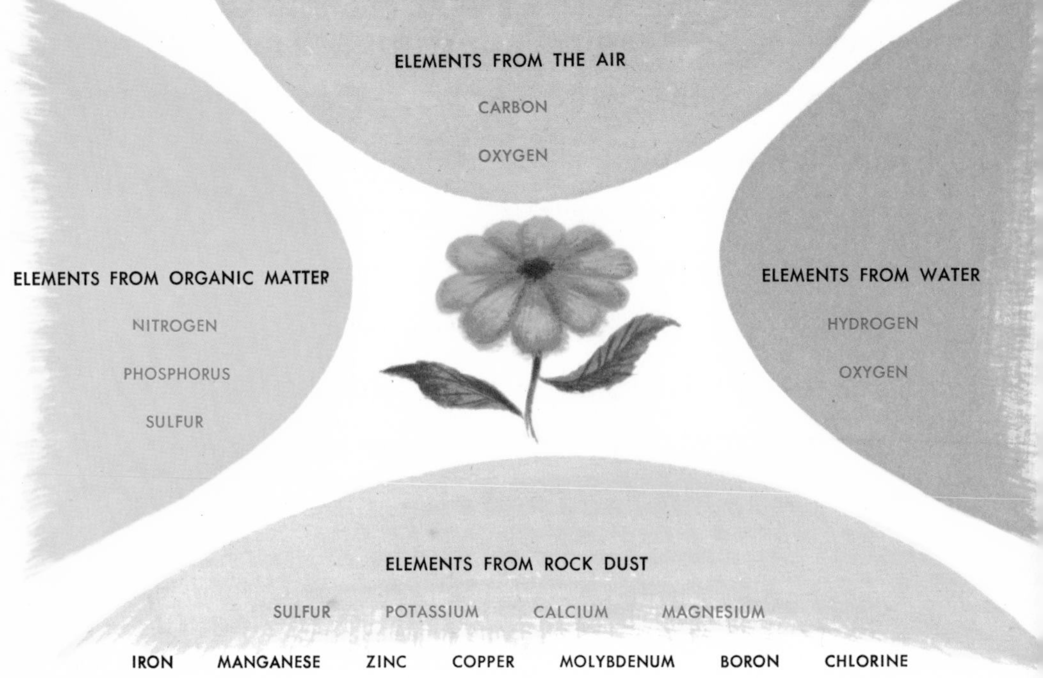

ELEMENTS FROM THE AIR

CARBON

OXYGEN

ELEMENTS FROM ORGANIC MATTER

NITROGEN

PHOSPHORUS

SULFUR

ELEMENTS FROM WATER

HYDROGEN

OXYGEN

ELEMENTS FROM ROCK DUST

| SULFUR | POTASSIUM | CALCIUM | MAGNESIUM |

| IRON | MANGANESE | ZINC | COPPER | MOLYBDENUM | BORON | CHLORINE |

Plants are made of chemical elements. Some of the elements that plants need come from the rock dust of the soil. Other elements come from the organic matter, the air, or from water.

The picture shows some of the chemical elements most needed by plants. The elements shown in red letters are the most important. The others are needed in smaller amounts.

14

Soil that has all of the chemical elements that plants need is said to be fertile.   Plants grow well in fertile soil.

In places where the soil lacks some of the chemical elements plants need, men may add some fertilizers.   A fertilizer may have many different plant-food elements in it.   Soil scientists help farmers find out what kind of fertilizer their soil needs.

1 Plants take chemical elements out of the soil as they grow.

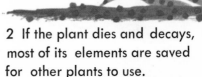

2 If the plant dies and decays, most of its elements are saved for other plants to use.

3 If the plant is taken away, the elements in it cannot return to the soil.

4 The farmer puts plant food into the soil to replace elements that are taken away.

Nitrogen is a chemical element that plants need very much.   But they cannot get it from the inorganic matter in the soil, or from the air.   The picture shows how plants get nitrogen through the nitrogen cycle.

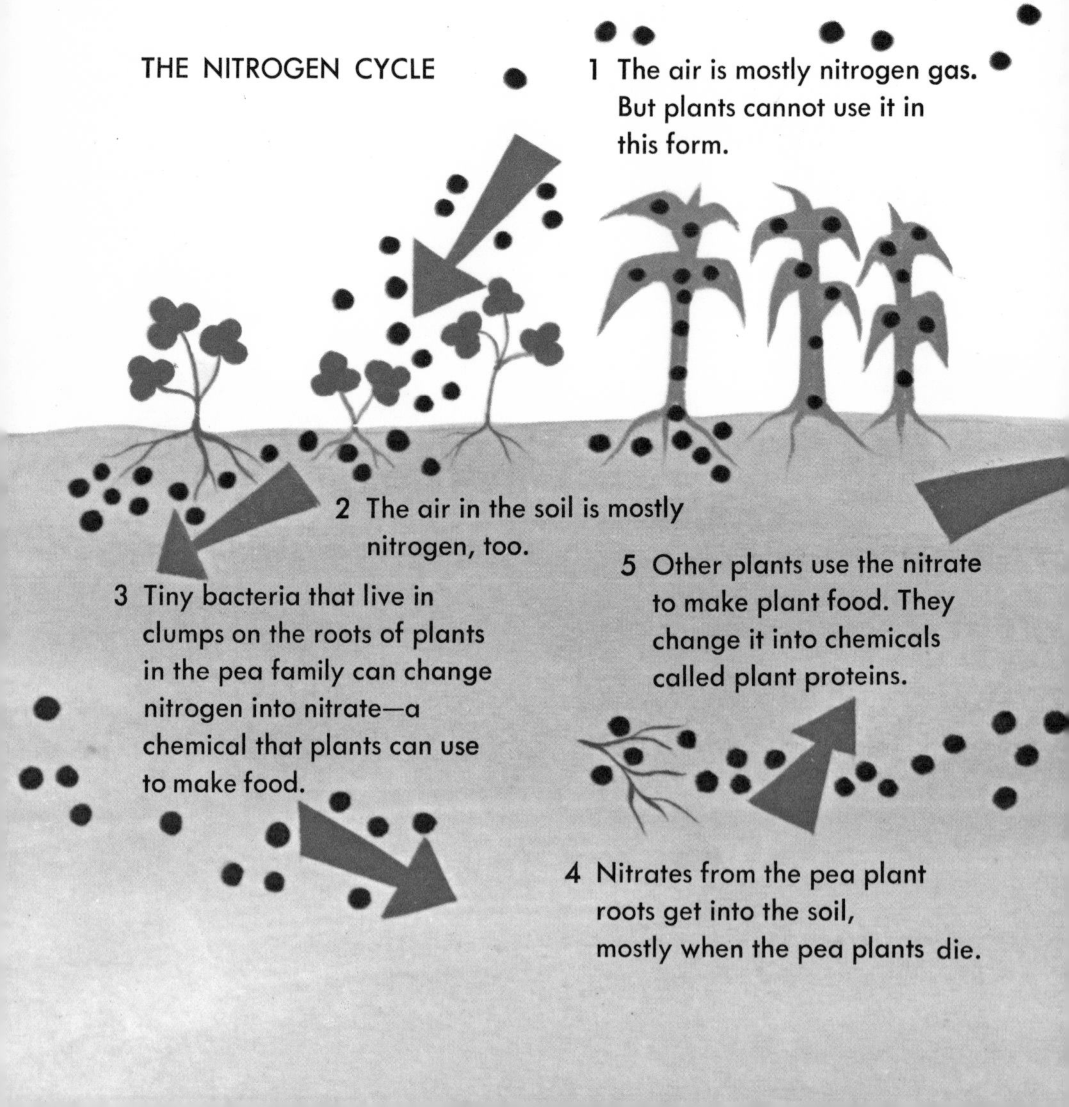

THE NITROGEN CYCLE

1 The air is mostly nitrogen gas. But plants cannot use it in this form.

2 The air in the soil is mostly nitrogen, too.

3 Tiny bacteria that live in clumps on the roots of plants in the pea family can change nitrogen into nitrate—a chemical that plants can use to make food.

5 Other plants use the nitrate to make plant food. They change it into chemicals called plant proteins.

4 Nitrates from the pea plant roots get into the soil, mostly when the pea plants die.

Nitrogen is added to the soil in another way, too.   Lightning heats the air and makes the nitrogen come together with oxygen gas in the air.   This new material, called a nitrogen compound, is picked up by raindrops.   The rain carries the nitrogen compound to the soil.

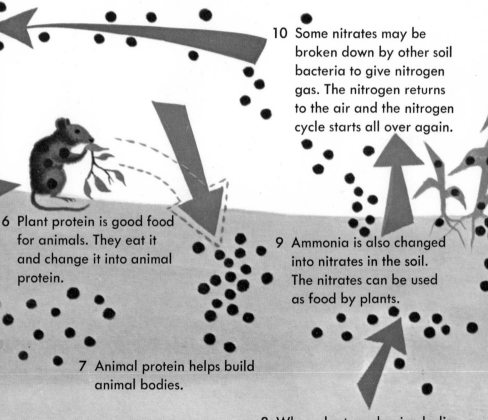

10 Some nitrates may be broken down by other soil bacteria to give nitrogen gas. The nitrogen returns to the air and the nitrogen cycle starts all over again.

6 Plant protein is good food for animals. They eat it and change it into animal protein.

9 Ammonia is also changed into nitrates in the soil. The nitrates can be used as food by plants.

7 Animal protein helps build animal bodies.

8 When plants and animals die, decay bacteria change their protein into another nitrogen chemical called ammonia.

There are many, many different kinds of soil in the world. Some soils are good for growing grain. Some are good for growing cotton. Other soils are suited for vegetables or fruit trees. A few soils are so poor that they grow nothing but weeds.

Some soil that is now almost useless for crops was once fertile.   Careless farming has spoiled this land.

Careful farmers take good care of their soil.   They keep it fertile so it will continue to grow good crops.

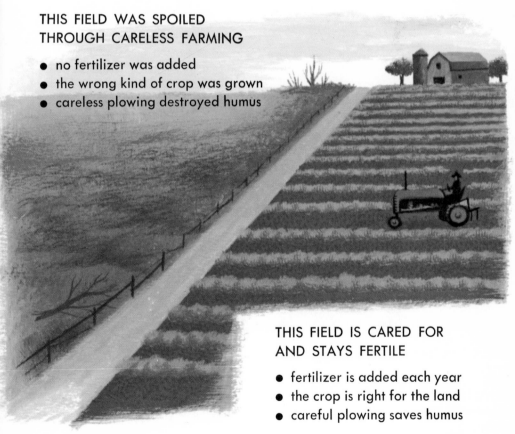

THIS FIELD WAS SPOILED
THROUGH CARELESS FARMING

- no fertilizer was added
- the wrong kind of crop was grown
- careless plowing destroyed humus

THIS FIELD IS CARED FOR
AND STAYS FERTILE

- fertilizer is added each year
- the crop is right for the land
- careful plowing saves humus

19

A young soil has most of its organic
matter near the top. Rain washes the
organic matter downward. After many
years, organic matter will be found
deeper in the soil.

Water changes the soil. Rain washes organic
matter and chemicals down from the topsoil into
the subsoil. This is called leaching. Leaching
happens very, very slowly in most places.

20

In places with heavy rainfall, too much leaching may carry chemicals down out of the reach of the plant roots.   It is hard to grow corn, grain, and other crops that need a lot of chemicals in a soil that is badly leached. Sometimes farmers add fertilizer to this soil.

Fertilizer is expensive. So sometimes it does not pay to grow corn or vegetables on leached soil that would need a lot of fertilizer. The land is used for grass instead.

Plants will not grow unless there is water in the soil. In places where the soil is fertile, but there is not much rain, men bring water to their farms in pipes or in ditches. This is called irrigation.

WITHOUT IRRIGATION
desert soil is good only for tough plants that do not need much water.

WITH IRRIGATION
some kinds of desert soil will grow good crops.

Winter vegetables are grown on
Florida land that used to be
marshy. Ditches carry the
extra water away to the sea.

In some places, the land holds water
instead of letting it drain away. The soil
becomes very wet, and the place is called a
marsh or a swamp. Most crops cannot grow in
a marsh. If men drain some of the extra water
out of the marsh, the soil can sometimes be
used for growing crops.

23

1 A raindrop strikes the soil
and breaks off pieces of it.

2 Some of the soil goes into
the water as it flows away.

3 Muddy water carries the
topsoil away from the land.

The washing away of the soil by moving
water is called water erosion.   Water erosion
destroys much good farmland in the world.   It
takes away the fertile topsoil.   All that is
left is the less fertile subsoil and soil parent
material.

A very hard rain causes the most water erosion damage. A freshly plowed field often suffers water erosion during a rainstorm.

Erosion happens in places where the soil is not covered with plants. After a farmer plows his field, the soil may lie bare until crops grow. Rain falls on the bare soil. Some of the water soaks into the soil, but the rest of it flows away. It takes some of the topsoil with it.

Planting vines helps cover the bare soil in a gully.

Logs and sticks slow down flowing water and trap mud.

Sometimes a small dam can hold back water and plug the gully.

Sometimes erosion can happen so slowly that the farmer hardly notices it. The topsoil will just get thinner and thinner.

But in other places, where the land is steep, erosion may make a gully. A gully looks just like a small canyon. It has very steep walls. Every time it rains, the walls of the gully crumble, and the gully gets bigger and bigger.

TERRACING is used on steep land.
The farmer makes bigger walls of
soil to catch and hold muddy water.

CONTOUR PLANTING makes little
walls at each row that trap
the water and mud as they flow
downhill.

COVER CROPS are plants with
roots that hold the soil.
They are planted on soil that
might otherwise be left bare.

STRIP FARMING means planting
strips of different crops. Some
crops prevent erosion better
than others.

Farmers must use the land carefully in
order to prevent water erosion.   The picture
shows some ways to do this.

Soil can also be damaged by wind erosion. This happens when men do not farm carefully in dry places. It also happens when animals eat most of the plants and leave bare soil. If the soil is left bare, a strong wind may blow the fertile topsoil away. Great dust storms of the past have destroyed many farms.

Trees on a hill help hold back soil when rain falls. If fire destroys the trees, rain can easily wash the soil away.

Fire is another great enemy of soil. Humus burns. Forest fires and grass fires burn up the humus and make the soil less fertile. When plants are destroyed, water and wind erosion are able to harm the soil still more.

Most farmers take good care
of the soil they have.

For many years, farmers in North America
were careless with the soil. It took a long
time for men to learn that they had to take
good care of the soil.

Now we know that we would not be able to
live without the soil. Most farmers study
soil science. They can grow more food today
than they ever could before.

Words Younger Children May Need Help With

(Numbers refer to page on which the word first appears.)

4	inorganic	9	climates	15	fertile
5	organic	10	glaciers		fertilizers
6	gravel	12	lichens	16	nitrogen
	silt		chemical		cycle
	mixture	13	decay	17	oxygen
7	topsoil		bacteria		compound
	subsoil		humus	19	continue
	parent		moisture	20	leaching
	material	14	elements	22	irrigation
8	weathering		amounts	24	erosion

THINGS TO DO IN SCHOOL OR AT HOME

Collect different kinds of soil. Use peanut butter jars with screw-on lids to hold soil samples that you collect. Paste a label on the outside of each jar telling where the soil was collected and what type of plants (grass, weeds, crops, evergreens, broadleaf trees) were growing in the soil. Try to obtain soil from a woodland, from an open field, from a marsh or pond bottom, from a roadside, and from a place where grass is growing well. Do the soil samples have the same color? Do they smell the same? Which samples have tiny animals in them? Look at a pinch of each kind of soil under a magnifying glass and then under a microscope. Are the soil particles from one sample all the same, or is the soil a mixture of many different materials?

Test your soil samples. Use small paper plates for this experiment. Write the name of the soil on each plate before you begin. Place a smooth layer of soil, about one-half inch deep, in the center of the plate. Pat it down well, then water it. Allow the soil to dry completely and see what it looks like. Did the soil crack? Did it get hard or remain soft enough to stir easily? Do you think young plants would do well in a soil that dried into a rock-hard material?

Why? Wet the soil again, and stir it up well while it is wet. Allow it to dry and see whether the stirring made the soil more likely to get hard and crack. Why do many farmers avoid plowing or cultivating their soils when the land is wet?

Chop up some leaves and grass into tiny pieces, dry them, and then mix them with your soil samples. Repeat the wetting experiment. Did you find that the soils were less likely to get hard when the organic material was mixed with them? How might a gardener improve a soil that turned rock-hard after it was wet and dried?

Grow plants in soil samples. Fill paper cups with soil at least 3½ inches deep. Use samples from your collection. Get a packet of seed corn and plant three kernels in each cup. See which kind of soil grows the tallest corn seedlings. (Don't forget to water the plants regularly and give them a sunny place to grow.)

Take some topsoil from your yard and place it in a cup. Dig deeper to obtain some subsoil, too. (It will be a different color, probably lighter than the topsoil.) Plant corn in both kinds of soil and see which plants look stronger and larger. Why must farmers be careful not to let their topsoil wash or blow away?

Obtain some fertilizer and mix a small amount with subsoil in one cup. One pinch should be enough. Bury one small sardine in the middle of the subsoil in another cup. Plant corn in both cups and see how the plants grow. Long ago, the Indians of certain tribes placed fish in the soil in which they planted their corn. Why? Do you think a farmer would be able to use fish in this way for fertilizer today? Look up the fish MENHADEN in the encyclopedia and see what it is used for.